Variations for Judith
for piano
(easy to intermediate)

11 short reflections on *Bist du bei mir*
G H Stölzel arr J S Bach

Richard Rodney Bennett
Michael Berkeley
Diana Burrell
Anthony Burton
Peter Maxwell Davies
Jonathan Dove
Stephen Johns
Thea Musgrave
Tarik O'Regan
Anthony Payne
Judith Weir

CHESTER MUSIC

The complete Variations for Judith was given its premiere at Spitalfields
Music Summer Festival on 18th June 2012 performed by Melvyn Tan.

Variations for Judith performed by Melvyn Tan is available on NMC Recordings.
Cat no. NMC DL3009 (mp3/FLAC only).
www.nmcrec.co.uk

Order No. CH75834
ISBN 978-1-84938-269-4

Music set by Robin Hagues

This edition © 2012 Chester Music Limited,
part of the Music Sales Group
Published in Great Britain

Head Office: 14/15 Berners Street, London W1T 3LJ

Tel +44 (0)20 7612 7400
Fax +44 (0)20 7612 7545

A proportion of proceeds from the sale of music and royalties of Variations for Judith are going
to Dimbleby Cancer Care, who support patients and carers, including Judith, through cancer treatment.
Dimbleby Cancer Care was set up following the death of broadcaster Richard Dimbleby in 1966. Since
then, through generous public donations, the charity has funded work in the field of cancer care and
cancer care research, including the Richard Dimbleby Laboratory at Kings College Hospital, the
Dimbleby Cancer Care and Information Services at Guy's and St Thomas' Hospital. The Dimbleby
Cancer Care Research Fund commissions research projects exploring different aspects of cancer care.

The charity relies on donations to continue its work and is delighted by the kind gift from the publishers
and composers of Variations for Judith. For more information, or to make a donation,
please visit www.dimblebycancercare.org

DIMBLEBY CANCER CARE
in memory of Richard Dimbleby

Introduction

When Judith Serota left the Spitalfields Festival after nearly twenty years at the helm, I felt a very special leaving present was required. There can be few people in the world whose love and enthusiasm for music exceeds Judith's, and knowing that she had recently become a keen student of the piano, I thought that a specially-written collection of new compositions for herself to play would seem an appropriate gift. I consequently approached all of the Spitalfields Festival Artistic Directors asking them to write a short variation; Chris Sayers chose the theme and, except for Richard Hickox who - far too modestly perhaps - felt his compositional skills were not up to the task, all of them enthusiastically set about composing pieces for Judith. As the variations began to land on my doormat, I could see that there was the making of a fine collection of eminently playable little gems. David Titterington produced the realisation of the original Stölzel tune immortalised by Bach, I chose an order for the variations and Judith was duly presented with her *Klavierbüchlein* after an excellent first performance by Andrew Blankfield at her leaving party on November 30th 2007.

Since then, four new "reflections" have been added to the collection. Tarik O'Regan was commissioned, Richard Rodney Bennett and Thea Musgrave premiered and Peter Maxwell Davies, who was the first composer Judith ever met, had work performed at Spitalfields Festival before she left in 2007.

The gift was made for Judith, but I hope it will also provide much joy and inspiration to all pianists who enjoy exploring something fresh and different.

Diana Burrell. Artistic Director, Spitalfields Festival, 2006 - 2009

Artistic Directors of the Spitalfields Festival:

- Richard Hickox (1990-1993) - though he took responsibility for the artistic direction of the Festival from 1976-1989
- Michael Berkeley and Anthony Payne (joint Artistic Directors 1995–1997)
- Judith Weir (joint 1995-1997, later sole Artistic Director 1998–2000)
- Stephen Johns (Guest Artistic Director Winter 2000)
- Anthony Burton (Guest Artistic Director Summer 2001)
- Jonathan Dove (Artistic Director 2001–2006)
- Diana Burrell (Artistic Director 2006–2009).

Variations for Judith
Bist du bei mir BWV 508

Realisation:
David Titterington (b. 1958)

from J.S. Bach: *Klavierbüchlein für Anna Magdalena Bach*

G.H. Stölzel
(1690–1749)

2

for Judith with admiration, affection and gratitude

I. Breaking Away

Anthony Burton
(b.1947)

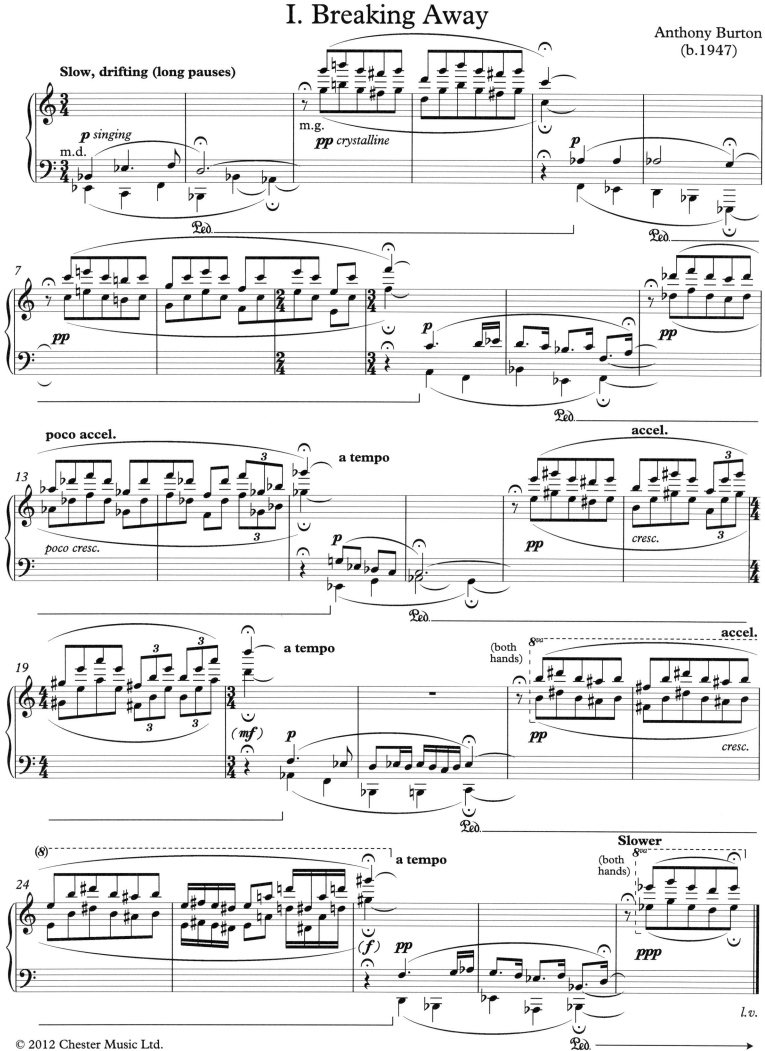

for Judith Serota with much love

II. Spitalfields Echoes

Stephen Johns
(b. 1964)

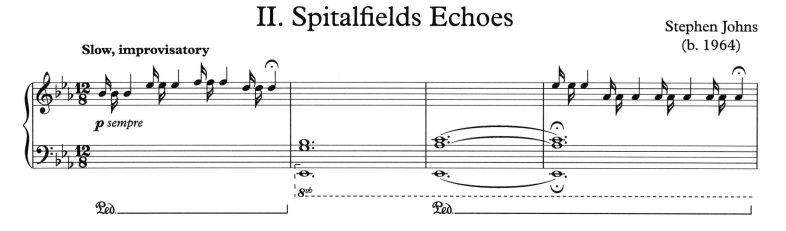

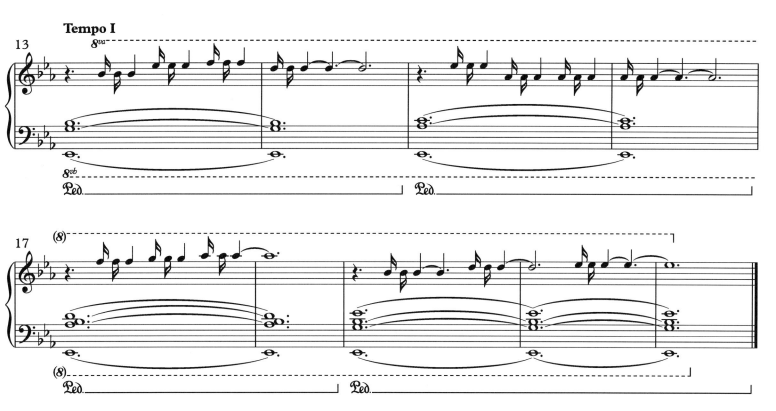

with affection and admiration

III. Loose Canon for Jude

Anthony Payne
(b. 1936)

for Judith – with much love

IV. Music for Judith

Diana Burrell
(b. 1948)

Strong, bright and always very lyrical ♩ = *c.*96

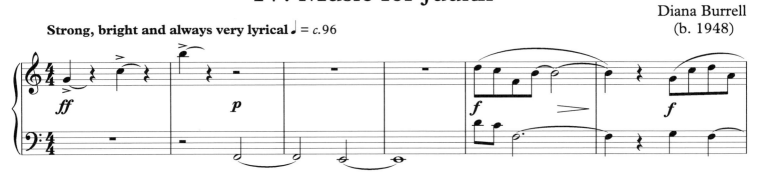

V. to Judith, from Judith

Judith Weir
(b. 1954)

Light and bright ♩ = *c.*112

VI. Little Elegy

Richard Rodney Bennett
(b. 1936)

for Judith

VII. Lullaby

Michael Berkeley
(b. 1948)

for Estela and all others bravely fighting cancer

VIII. Prelude

Thea Musgrave
(b. 1928)

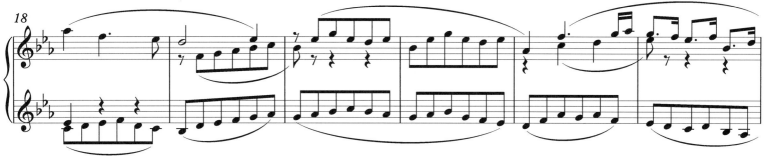

poco rit.

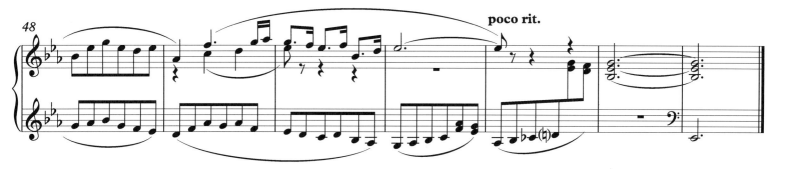

for Judith Serota

IX. Diomedes

Tarik O'Regan
(b. 1978)

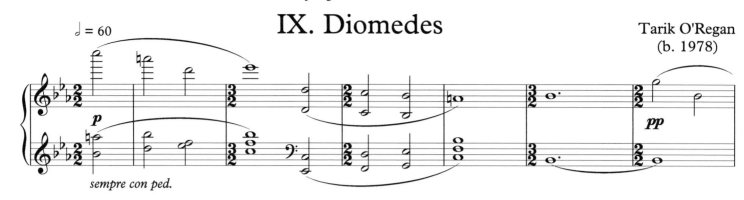

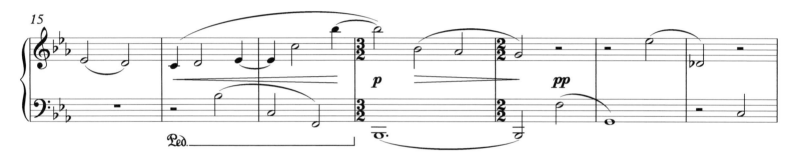

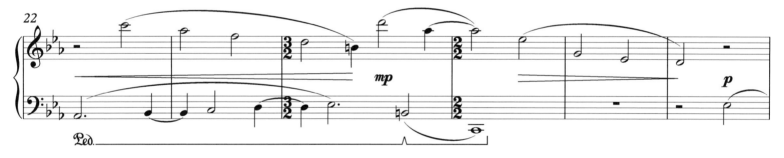

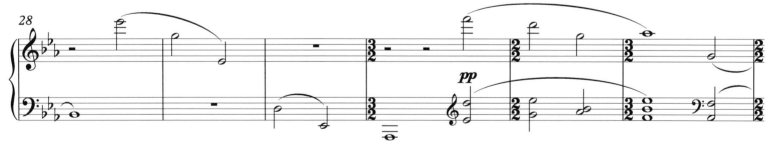

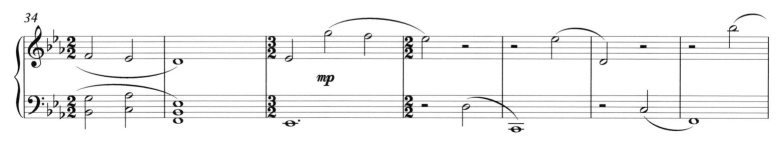

'Bist du bei mir' is an aria originally from Stölzel's opera *Diomedes oder die triumphierende Unschuld.*
Diomedes is one of my favourite characters in the Iliad and Aeneid. There's something very robust,
but gentle about him – characteristics I wanted to bring out in the piece ...

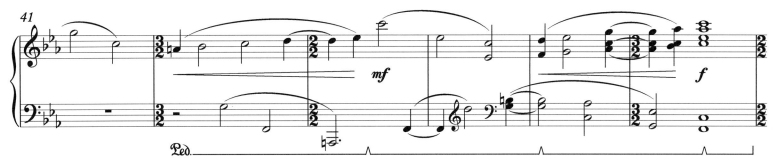

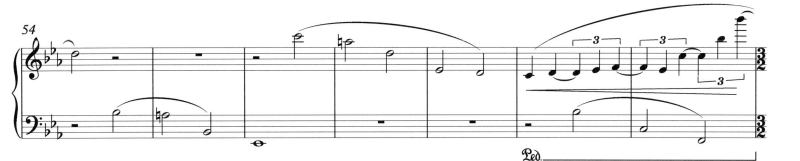

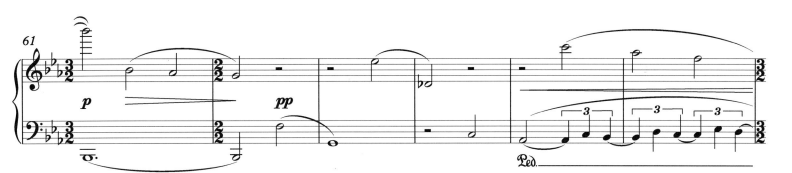

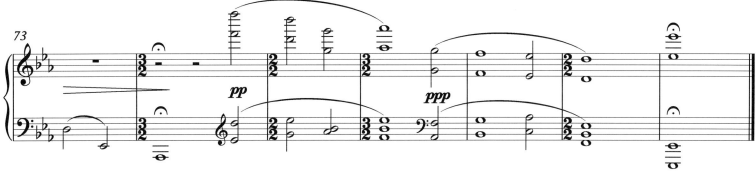

for Judith

X. Ist Bach bei mir

Jonathan Dove
(b. 1959)

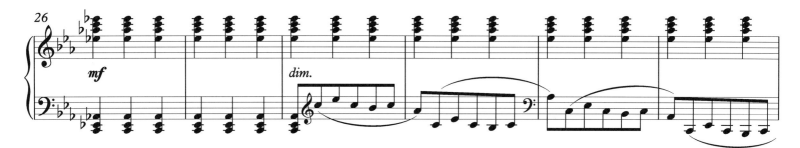

for Judith Serota

XI. Bist du bei mir... oder?

Peter Maxwell Davies
after G. H. Hölzel
(b. 1934)

Adagio con fantasia ♩ = *c.*54

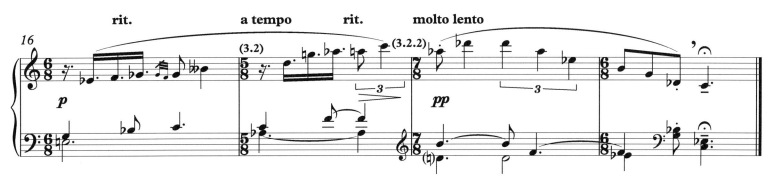